COUNCIL*on*
FOREIGN
RELATIONS

Center for Preventive Action

Discussion Paper
September 2022

Climate Change and Regional Instability in Central America

Prospects for Internal Disorder, Human Mobility, and Interstate Tensions

Paul J. Angelo

The Council on Foreign Relations (CFR) is an independent, nonpartisan membership organization, think tank, and publisher dedicated to being a resource for its members, government officials, business executives, journalists, educators and students, civic and religious leaders, and other interested citizens in order to help them better understand the world and the foreign policy choices facing the United States and other countries. Founded in 1921, CFR carries out its mission by maintaining a diverse membership, including special programs to promote interest and develop expertise in the next generation of foreign policy leaders; convening meetings at its headquarters in New York and in Washington, DC, and other cities where senior government officials, members of Congress, global leaders, and prominent thinkers come together with CFR members to discuss and debate major international issues; supporting a Studies Program that fosters independent research, enabling CFR scholars to produce articles, reports, and books and hold roundtables that analyze foreign policy issues and make concrete policy recommendations; publishing *Foreign Affairs*, the preeminent journal of international affairs and U.S. foreign policy; sponsoring Independent Task Forces that produce reports with both findings and policy prescriptions on the most important foreign policy topics; and providing up-to-date information and analysis about world events and American foreign policy on its website, CFR.org.

The Council on Foreign Relations takes no institutional positions on policy issues and has no affiliation with the U.S. government. All views expressed in its publications and on its website are the sole responsibility of the author or authors.

For further information about CFR or this paper, please write to the Council on Foreign Relations, 58 East 68th Street, New York, NY 10065, or call Communications at 212.434.9888. Visit CFR's website, CFR.org.

This Discussion Paper was made possible by a grant from the Carnegie Corporation of New York. The statements made and views expressed are solely the responsibility of the author.

CONTENTS

INTRODUCTION

With more than 1.7 million encounters reported by U.S. Customs and Border Protection—the highest tally in two decades—2021 was an exceptional year for irregular migration to the U.S. southern border. Although that number includes citizens from at least 121 countries, some 43 percent of those apprehended by U.S. authorities hailed from Central America.[1]

For more than a decade, migration from Mexico's southern neighbors was on the rise, but the COVID-19 pandemic and associated economic recession triggered unprecedented levels of cross-border flow, prompting the Joe Biden administration to prioritize U.S. programs aimed at addressing the socioeconomic, political, and security drivers of migration. In the process, the Biden administration refocused the U.S. government's efforts to factor climate change risks as catalysts for regional displacement. Indeed, the effects of climate change on migration could no longer be ignored after back-to-back category 4 and category 5 hurricanes, Eta and Iota, pummeled the Caribbean coast of Central America in November 2020. The ruin left by the two cyclones gave rise to a new period of climate-induced instability in Central America.

In addition to extreme weather events, irregular precipitation patterns, deforestation, and high temperatures increasingly contribute to upended livelihoods and rampant food insecurity. From 2018 to 2021, the number of people going hungry in Central America nearly quadrupled, topping out at close to eight million.[2] A 2017 study ranked Guatemala, Honduras, and Nicaragua among the ten countries in the world most vulnerable to climate-based risks, with those living along the Pacific Coast in the region's Dry Corridor especially susceptible.[3]

The Notre Dame Global Adaptation Initiative, a leading research program that ranks countries by their preparedness for addressing climate vulnerability, listed the countries of Central America among the worst performers in the world due to the magnitude of challenges and the incapacity of regional governments to respond, with Honduras taking the group's lowest position at 139 out of 182 countries assessed.[4] Despite contributing less than 0.2 percent of global carbon emissions, the low-income countries of Central America shoulder a disproportionate environmental burden imposed by the world's most prosperous and carbon-emitting countries.[5]

Barring massive shifts in policy and human behavior around the world, environmental degradation due to climate change will fuel volatility in Central America for decades to come, with disruptive spillover effects for neighboring Mexico and the United States. Halting the flow of people northward from Central America is neither feasible nor desirable, especially given growing labor demands in the United States and Mexico. But ensuring migration remains an option, not a necessity, requires long-range planning and international cooperation to alleviate the impending climate fallout.

THE EFFECTS OF CLIMATE CHANGE IN CENTRAL AMERICA

Poverty, inequality, unemployment, corruption, and violent crime have all contributed to the exodus of people from Central America in the past decade, revealing the importance of human security, or the security of people and communities rather than the security of states, for addressing the root causes of migration from the region. After all, freedom from fear, want, and indignity—as the human security concept prescribes—encompasses the enduring security concerns of the region's inhabitants, who have not experienced interstate conflict since 1969 and have enjoyed nearly three decades of relative peace after putting an end to Cold War insurgencies in the 1990s.[6]

Yet, for too long, U.S. policymakers have decoupled the development needs of Central Americans from their increased vulnerability to climate-induced environmental hazards. As early as 2014, the Pentagon's Quadrennial Defense Review identified climate change as a global "threat multiplier," but U.S. foreign assistance aimed at reducing Central American instability missed an opportunity to address how climate change interacts with other destabilizing environmental, socioeconomic, and political factors.[7] That same year, the Barack Obama administration launched a new U.S. Strategy for Engagement in Central America that prioritized three lines of action—promoting prosperity and regional integration, strengthening governance, and improving security. However, of the $750 million approved by Congress for the 2016 fiscal year for northern Central America—the countries of El Salvador, Guatemala, and Honduras—the U.S. Agency for International Development (USAID) devoted a mere $70 million to building community resilience aimed at countering the effects of climate change in the region.[8]

Part of the challenge in tackling the consequences of climate change in Central America is the lack of climate data. Historical temperature data, which would indicate sharper rises in annual average temperatures, is often not available for more remote, rural areas of regional countries. Likewise, to identify rainfall trends, scientists require centuries' worth of data, but Central American governments possess records dating back only a few decades. Although scientists agree that the region is facing unprecedented difficulties due to shifts in demography and climate, a broader lack of consensus on causality and whether anything can be done locally to turn back a global phenomenon has resulted in limited and belated strategies—ones that emphasize adaptation rather than mitigation. Even then, regional governments severely underinvest in adaptation measures due to budgetary constraints and competing development challenges.

Changes in temperature and precipitation are exacerbating already fragile environmental, socioeconomic, and political conditions in Central America, fueling heightened internal disorder, displacement, and tensions among governments. In turn, Central Americans are abandoning their homes, traditional livelihoods, and civic responsibilities in droves, seeking relief, work, and rights in the United States, Mexico, and other industrialized countries.

ENVIRONMENTAL CONDITIONS

Climate has presented unique challenges to the region's inhabitants since its settlement more than four millennia ago.[9] Today's inhabitants confront many of the same environmental conditions as their ancestors but on a much greater scale given population growth, unsustainable lifestyle patterns, and the increased frequency of extreme climate events. Warming waters in the Pacific Ocean affect wind patterns, raising temperatures in coastal wetlands and contributing to increasing frequency and intensity of dry spells, a phenomenon known regionally as El Niño Southern Oscillation. Conversely, in the Caribbean Sea, higher water temperatures prompt more rainfall and a higher incidence of tropical storms and cyclones, often resulting in flash flooding and landslides. In 2020, flooding astonishingly affected more than half of Honduras's population.[10]

Historically, the prevalence of extreme weather patterns heightened the risk of erosion of arable and habitable land. Some areas of Central America have proven more vulnerable to these challenges, and erosion, desertification, and deforestation have especially afflicted populations occupying the Dry Corridor, a tropical dry forest region particularly vulnerable to drought and irregular rains spanning from Costa Rica to southern Mexico. To this day, colonial-era land tenure arrangements, which concentrated the region's poorest smallholders along this stretch of territory, reproduce the environmental—not to mention, economic—marginalization of Central America's rural labor force.

Higher water temperatures in the Caribbean Sea have also induced unprecedented coral bleaching in the world's second-largest barrier reef, which runs from Mexico's Yucatan Peninsula along the coasts of Belize, Guatemala, and Honduras. Heat stress reduces algae concentrations required to give coral their color and health, leading to a devastating and largely irreversible process of coral dieback. With conservative projections suggesting the loss of at least 70 percent of the world's coral reefs by 2050, Central America stands to endure untold marine destruction in the decades to come, adversely affecting food staples for coastal populations, fishing economies, and a growing tourism sector. Furthermore, as sea levels rise and alter coastlines, flooding and saline intrusion are damaging mangrove swamps, wetlands, and estuaries that are home to significant fish stocks and freshwater reserves.

Temperature increases and irregular rainfall have also resulted in vegetation die-off in Central American cloud forests, reducing natural water storage, harming biodiversity, and even contributing to amphibian extinctions.[11] Shifting climate patterns have contributed to more and longer forest fires and are potentially to blame for outbreaks of tree diseases, such as the pine bark beetle (*gorgojo del pino*) that destroyed Guatemalan and Honduran pine forests in 2019.[12] The increasing prevalence of plant disease has even affected Central America's most important cash crop, coffee. Although the coffee leaf rust fungus (*la roya*) affects regional coffee production annually, the 2012–13 harvest faced an especially damaging epidemic due to extreme temperatures, with the fungus reaching crops at higher altitudes than previously recorded and resulting in a 57 percent reduction in coffee production in Guatemala alone.[13] In a recent survey of Honduran producers, 95 percent of households indicated that climate change has impacted coffee production.[14]

Human behavior in Central America has exacerbated the region's overall environmental risk. El Salvador's history of deforestation to support a thriving indigo industry during the Spanish colonial era laid the groundwork for the country's heightened climate vulnerability. After centuries of clearing forests, El Salvador today has the lowest percentage of original forests per square mile of any country in the Americas, rendering its inhabitants especially vulnerable to landslides.[15] In Guatemala and Honduras, high deforestation to produce palm oil, livestock, bananas, and sugar cane accelerates soil erosion, reduces the sanitation of natural water sources, and shortens rainfall periods.

Human-induced environmental devastation also extends to protected marine zones. In these coastal areas, the deposit of human waste and mining and agricultural runoff could be linked to fatal diseases that have taken hold in Caribbean sea urchin, sponge, and coral populations.[16] Higher water temperatures have also led to an explosion of sargassum seaweed coverage in coastal regions of the Caribbean, polluting once-pristine beaches with the foul-smelling algae and, thus, deterring tourism. And Central America's considerable mangrove habitats—which sequester carbon, reduce water pollution, and dissipate coastal storm surges—face tremendous strain as local communities rely on them for fuelwood and timber, while coastal tourism, agriculture, and transportation infrastructure are rapidly taking their place.[17]

Climate change and local human activity are accelerating environmental degradation in Central America, inducing considerable stress on fragile ecosystems and provoking irreversible damage to the region's topography. Without major interventions to reverse this destruction and mitigate its effects, permanent environmental disaster in Central America is not a question of *if* but *when*.

SOCIOECONOMIC CONDITIONS

Given Central America's reliance on agriculture as a driver of economic growth, changes in land tenure due to climate change stand to upset the region's economic base. Environmental degradation as a result of rising temperatures and variable precipitation patterns is already resulting in economic, educational, and health precarity and rising social tensions—trends that promise to worsen as climate stress hastens.

Central America's major subsistence crops—maize, beans, rice, and sorghum—are rainfed; the food security of many of the region's inhabitants depends on stable climatic conditions.[18] But the unpredictability of the planting season due to the variability and occasional prolongation of the *canícula*, the summer heat wave that occurs between two annual harvests, has contributed to repeated crop losses. In recent years, prolonged droughts due to climate change have resulted in drastically reduced subsistence agriculture yield, plunging millions of Central Americans into poverty and malnutrition.[19]

From 2014 to 2015, an especially persistent period of drought contributed to food insecurity for more than half a million families in El Salvador, Guatemala, Honduras, and Nicaragua. During this period, a lack of rainfall in the summer months depleted 75 percent of subsistence crops in some regions.[20] Declining availability of food is not only a problem inland. Combined with coral dieback and the destruction of mangrove swamps that devastated once-thriving local fisheries on the coasts, these conditions pushed the number of food insecure people in the four countries to eight million in 2021.[21]

Food insecurity exacerbates malnutrition, contributing to adverse health outcomes for the region's youngest inhabitants. Although the last two decades have seen a decrease in stunting—the impaired growth and development of children as a result of poor nutrition—in Central America and Mexico, the subregion still has the highest prevalence of this phenomenon in the Americas, affecting 16.6 percent of children under five.[22] Notably, Guatemala has the fifth highest rate of stunting in the world, reaching around 70 percent in the country's western highlands.[23] In addition to physical growth, malnutrition affects children's acquisition of cognitive skills, mortality rates, and lifetime morbidities. It also leads to lower educational attainment and a loss of productive capacity.[24] School attendance in Central America is well below the Latin American average, with fewer than 40 percent of young people in northern Central America completing secondary education.[25] This trend is especially noticeable among low-income communities, including vulnerable racial and ethnic groups. According to the World Bank, a child born in Honduras today will be 48 percent as productive as they would be if they benefited from a complete secondary education and full health.[26]

In addition to impairing child development, changing weather patterns undermine public health outcomes across all demographics. Heat stress is linked to dehydration, chronic kidney disease, respiratory and cardiovascular conditions, asthma, and rhinitis.[27] During the wet season, the contamination of water supplies in low-lying regions due to a lack of water filtration systems and persistent flooding denies many inhabitants publicly available drinking water. Additionally, the incidence of vector-borne disease in these areas increases as temperatures rise, causing mosquitoes to become infectious more quickly. The 2014–15 El Niño phenomenon, for instance, amplified a regional Zika virus outbreak.[28] The Guatemalan capital and highlands, which previously did not experience dengue epidemics, have seen several such outbreaks during heat waves in recent years.[29]

Beyond health challenges, drought is also affecting Central America's important agribusiness sector, which employs between 20 and 40 percent of the working population in northern Central America and Nicaragua.[30] In the Dry Corridor, water-intensive export crops such as avocados, melons, and grapes are failing due to inadequate rainfall and inattention to retaining water.[31] And as agricultural plots move to higher elevations to accommodate more favorable conditions, the contamination and overuse of upstream water sources also harm downstream crops, including sugar plantations in coastal areas that serve as important employers of regional seasonal labor.

Overall, changes in employment affect not only food production but also the capacity of Central Americans to buy the food they cannot produce. The 2013 coffee rust crisis led to an estimated $1 billion in coffee crop losses and the loss of 100,000 jobs.[32] Even before the devastating effects of Eta and Iota, around half of Honduras's population lived in poverty, with more than a quarter living in extreme poverty; poverty rates in Central America crept even higher during the COVID-19 pandemic.[33] Job scarcity, particularly in the formal sector, tends to exacerbate the living conditions of historically marginalized communities such as women, Indigenous people, and Afro-descendants.[34]

Finally, the energy potential of most Central American countries, which depend on hydropower to meet national energy needs, is at risk as riverbeds dry up and water runoff declines. Central Americans experience regular prolonged power outages, and existing energy insecurity adversely affects everything from the physical conditions of housing and hospitals to family expenditures and productive capacity. This burden falls disproportionately on the region's most impoverished, reinforcing socioeconomic exclusion that drives discontent.

POLITICAL CONDITIONS

Political stability depends on social and economic stability, which Central America has long lacked due to inequitable access to land and natural resources. The region's Cold War–era civil wars were waged in large part over a historically exploitative land tenure system. Despite an end to the fighting, land distribution in the region remains highly unequal and contentious. In the most severe case, the wealthiest 2.5 percent of Guatemala's farmers possess nearly two-thirds of arable terrain, while some 90 percent of farms are concentrated on a mere one-sixth of the agricultural land.[35] Climate change and environmental degradation raise the costs of doing business, as productive land becomes scarce and expensive adaptive measures increase startup capital costs. This scenario, in turn, foments intra-societal competition, driving discord and affecting political outcomes.

Globally, climate change is a "contingent public liability" that is straining government finances.[36] In northern Central America and Nicaragua, extreme weather events caused more than $16 billion in economic losses from 1982 to 2011.[37] Low tax revenues already constrain government spending, which translates into low investments in social protection and infrastructure.[38] Thus, a majority of citizens in El Salvador, Guatemala, and Honduras harbor skepticism about the management of public budgets and a broader distrust of political authorities.[39] Throughout the region, the private sector, international donors, and citizens (often buttressed by remittances from abroad) assume the bulk of the financial burden incurred by climate adaptation or post-disaster reconstruction. Small farm and business owners face the most considerable obstacles in this regard, as changing crops, fortifying physical structures, investing in alternative energy, and securing a steady water supply require access to credit and technical assistance.

The inability to remain economically self-sufficient—let alone, competitive—ultimately pushes smallholders off their farms and into cities. The urban communities that absorb many of these internally displaced individuals are themselves precarious, and new arrivals face ostracization, predatory violence, and gang recruitment.

In some areas of Central America, resource competition has also resulted in repression and the violent displacement of communities. Plans to build an interoceanic canal in Nicaragua prompted the Daniel Ortega administration to nationalize tracts of land in protected reserves inhabited by autonomously governed Indigenous communities. The Hong Kong Nicaragua Development company leading the project even admitted that some 35,000 farmers would have to be relocated to accommodate the massive infrastructure undertaking.[40] Between 2014 and 2017, thousands of Nicaraguans marched against the government's takeover of their ancestral lands, repeatedly clashing with security forces.[41] The canal's construction has been put on pause indefinitely, but Nicaraguan authorities continue to intimidate communities and expropriate their land, destroying local fisheries and forests while purportedly redistributing plots to loyalists of the ruling Sandinista Party for the development of vacation homes and livestock ranches.[42]

In the highly fertile Bajo Aguán region of neighboring Honduras—
"a laboratory for all kinds of conflicts" due to competition over the
area's natural wealth—authorities and private security forces have
evicted hundreds of smallholders to make way for large African palm
plantations and more recently an iron oxide mine.[43] In the wake of the
country's 2009 coup, as many as 150 activists seeking to reclaim land
through legal action and unlawful land occupations have been murdered.[44] Efforts to preserve the country's natural resources in the western region have also proven fatal. In 2016, environmental defender and
Goldman Prize recipient Berta Cáceres was murdered for opposing the
construction of the Agua Zarca Dam on the Gualcarque River, inciting
demonstrations for justice that shut down many of the country's transportation and commercial arteries for weeks. In 2020 alone, seventeen
land and environmental activists were killed in Honduras. As of 2022,
most of their cases remain unresolved.[45]

Endemic corruption and governmental indifference in Central
America intensify the worst effects of climate change. Outdated and
weakly enforced construction regulations stymie the building of more
resilient infrastructure. In Honduras, the national building code does
not stipulate electrical and sanitary requirements, denote safety considerations that account for environmental or climate risks, or restrict
construction in areas that are geologically unsound.[46] In one infamous
incident in Tegucigalpa in 2013, more than two hundred families lost
their homes when a landslide destroyed their recently constructed
community; the building permits had been issued without an associated seismic and geological survey.[47] And in San Pedro Sula, residents
of informal settlements along the banks of the city's rivers watched
as successive hurricanes washed away their belongings and homes in
2020. The memory of that tragedy, however, did not stop people from
rebuilding in the same flood zone after the water receded, and government authorities have not interceded to halt ongoing construction in
the affected areas.[48]

Weak rule of law, against a backdrop of land competition, has
also incentivized criminal activities with deleterious environmental effects. Drug-trafficking organizations often launder money in
land-intensive industries such as cattle ranching, large-scale farm-
ing, and timber. These activities fuel the deforestation of protected
natural reserves, with authorities turning a blind eye in exchange for
bribes. In Nicaragua, drug-linked deforestation represented nearly a
third of the country's total deforestation from 2001 to 2013.[49] These

logged tracts of land also serve as waypoints for drug shipments transiting the Central American isthmus after departing South America, and there is growing evidence that Guatemala and Honduras are now playing host to their own coca plantations, bringing drug precursors even closer to the U.S. market.[50]

In effect, climate change is inducing scarcity into the economies of Central America, disturbing the social peace, amplifying government dysfunction, and driving further environmental destruction. For many Central Americans, environmental protection goes beyond stewardship of the global commons: it is a matter of both identity and survival—with sweeping consequences for political conditions throughout the region.

CLIMATE-RELATED INSTABILITY THROUGH 2040

Central America has long been marked by instability, but climate change is exacerbating the environmental, socioeconomic, and political challenges that confront the region. Despite decades of sustained economic growth and expanding (albeit weak) democratic governance, the region has failed to retool society for altered weather patterns. This, in turn, creates demographic stresses that inflame the population's existing challenges.

Looking ahead roughly twenty years, intensified climate variability and a higher frequency of severe weather events will combine with population growth and surging urbanization to strain government capacity and worsen quality of life. Even the expected population growth of just above 1 percent, a modest figure by international standards, will leave increasing numbers of people vulnerable. In Guatemala, the urban population is expected to double by 2040. El Salvador, currently the forty-fifth most densely populated country in the world, will experience a concentration of 324.5 people per square kilometer by the same year.[51] This latter figure is significantly above the projected Latin American average of 36.9 in 2040—and augurs an especially challenging period of intra-societal competition.[52] And because regional governments have mostly assumed a reactive strategy for dealing with climate fallout to date, they are unlikely to commit substantially to mitigation and adaptation measures.

Although the prospect of interstate tensions in Central America due to climate change will remain moderate, shifting weather patterns and continued environmental degradation will exacerbate living conditions for Central Americans, leading to a high incidence of internal disorder, internal displacement, and outward migration.

INTERNAL DISORDER

Climate change will heighten resource competition and, thus, magnify existing socioeconomic challenges. In particular, population growth in Central America, combined with continued reductions in subsistence crop yield, will constrain the region's ability to meet food demand.[53] The high commodity prices driven by Russia's invasion of Ukraine in 2022 were a wake-up call for Central American governments, as poor households in the Dry Corridor faced extreme food insecurity until the late-summer harvest.[54] Yet authorities routinely rely on occasional subsidies and international assistance as stop-gap measures in these scenarios. They are severely inattentive to addressing food insecurity sustainably. Although the U.S. Department of Agriculture predicts declining food insecurity for Central America by 2031, the analytical model depends on macroeconomic stability, rising incomes, deeper integration into global supply chains, and relatively stable food prices— conditions that are anything but guaranteed if the region's history and recent events are a guide.[55]

To meet Central America's needs in ways that minimize exposure to external shocks, farmers will need to diversify their output and will require more arable land to sustain production. This reality should drive innovation and transformation in the agricultural sector, but it could also accelerate trends that further deteriorate soil conditions and rainfall such as deforestation. The agrarian crisis could quickly become an ecological catastrophe.

By 2040, environmental conditions will no longer support the current cultivation levels of some crops, including coffee, causing additional competition for limited cultivation areas, loss of biodiversity, accelerated erosion, and the outbreak of land conflicts.[56] Additionally, by 2100, freshwater availability is projected to decline by 88 percent in Honduras, 82 percent in Guatemala, and 73 percent in El Salvador due to the growing need for upstream irrigation.[57] Coastal communities, in particular, will bear the brunt of poor water resource management, as rising sea levels will continue to degrade coastal aquifers that open to the ocean.[58]

Unless energy grids are modernized, they will fail to keep pace with consumer demand. At current rates of rainfall fluctuations, temperature rise, and regional infrastructure investment, hydropower capacity in Mexico and Central America could face up to a 30 percent reduction by 2060.[59] Primary and secondary energy production has historically remained below total annual consumption in Central America. The precipitous rise in petroleum prices in 2022 led to protests from transportation workers and farmers from Guatemala to Panama, reflecting the region's vast dependency on energy imports. Despite nascent efforts to promote diversified renewable energy, hydropower and petroleum remain the principal sources of regional electrification, rendering Central Americans susceptible to rising global energy prices, higher transaction costs, and prolonged blackouts at home.[60]

In addition to constraining access to survival and quality-of-life resources, climate change will further expose deficiencies in governance and the rule of law. Pervasive distrust toward government is already fueling disaffection with democracy, and continued high unemployment, social resentment, and corruption will create additional opportunities for criminals to exert territorial control and reinforce their legitimacy as alternative service providers to populations that fall beyond government reach. This was the case in Central America during the COVID-19 pandemic, when gangs and cartels enforced lockdowns, distributed hand sanitizer and face masks, and delivered food to populations in need.

As environmental degradation extinguishes livelihoods and renders land inhospitable, people will become increasingly vulnerable to recruitment, extortion, and trafficking by nonstate armed groups. And worryingly, regional governments have historically dealt with these threats in ways that replicate violence: confrontational and repressive domestic policies known as the *mano dura* (hard-handed) approach to fighting gangs.

By 2040, climate change will generate additional food insecurity due to competition for arable land, water, and energy resources.

Improper resource management by regional governments also stands to generate new opportunities for criminal groups, inflaming a dire humanitarian crisis of societal violence. Accounting for these trends, Central America exhibits a high probability of internal disorder related to climate change.

INTERNAL DISPLACEMENT AND INTERNATIONAL MIGRATION

The mass movement of people is a reaction to two kinds of climate events—sudden-onset and slow-onset disasters. Hurricanes Eta and Iota are unmistakable examples of storms provoking sudden-onset migration, but other sporadic climate events such as wildfires and floods have produced unexpected displacement in recent years. On the other hand, slow-onset migration responds to disasters that pose a cumulative drain on livelihoods and life prospects, including sea-level rise, salinization, desertification, and erosion. In the past decade, Central Americans have been leaving their homes in record numbers due to a rising incidence of both.

During a recent prolonged drought associated with El Niño, only 11 percent of displaced individuals in Honduras departed for international destinations, suggesting that many Central Americans continue to seek opportunities in their own countries.[61] Indeed, from the rural areas of the Dry Corridor, where 80 percent of the 11 million residents live below the poverty line and where 62 percent depend on subsistence crops, noteworthy internal migration is already underway.[62]

A lasting consequence of the continuous depopulation of the countryside is uncontrolled urbanization. Today nearly six in ten Central Americans live in a city—a figure expected to rise to seven in ten for the next generation, as the region's urban population swells to double its current size by 2050.[63] Underinvestment in infrastructure and inattention to zoning have relegated new urban dwellers to persistent marginalization, and "more concrete means more flooding," as soil degradation reduces the ground's ability to absorb moisture.[64] Many internal migrants inhabit urban slums, lacking access to basic services and physical and digital connectivity. As it stands, around 40 percent of all city residents in Honduras and Nicaragua reside in such informal housing settlements.[65]

Under these mounting stresses, persistent human precarity translates into mass human migration. After all, internal displacement is a primary risk factor for international migration.[66] But in countries with no shortage of development challenges, human mobility is multicausal; climate change fails to tell the whole story when it comes to international migration. El Salvador and Honduras claimed the highest murder rates in the world in the mid-2010s, highlighting the scourge of criminal violence from rising gang recruitment and drug trafficking.[67] Furthermore, family reunification has long spurred cross-border movement, owing to a Central American–born population in the United States that has grown to at least four million, a more than tenfold increase since 1980.[68] Likewise, a recent survey of repatriated migrants finds that 92 percent of respondents in El Salvador, Guatemala, and Honduras identified economic reasons as their motive for leaving their countries.[69] A majority of the working population in Central America—over 80 percent in Nicaragua—is employed in the informal sector, which often means poor working conditions, underpayment, and a high risk of job redundancy owing to medical conditions, disability, and old age.[70]

Although the average migrant's decision to leave Central America responds to multiple push factors, climate change, if not a proximate cause of migration, still figures into many migrant narratives, especially following sudden-onset events.[71] Although families could leave their farms and look to migrate internally because of environmental degradation, the lack of safe or viable places within their country owing to other adverse conditions such as violence or unemployment tends to push them beyond their national borders. In a November 2021 survey of Central American households in which at least one member relocated, 85 percent left for international destinations.[72] As one recent study finds, decreases in rainfall in Honduras are associated with increases in family unit apprehensions at the U.S. southern border.[73] And among Guatemalans repatriated from the United States in 2021, U.S. officials noticed a stark rise in returnees from Alta Verapaz and Petén Departments, the two regions most affected by the 2020 hurricane season.[74]

Looking ahead to 2040, both internal and international migration will increase as climate change becomes more severe and its effects intertwine with existing development challenges. Rural-to-urban movement will accelerate as desertification and sea-level rise make currently populated zones unproductive or uninhabitable. A combination of slow-onset events and the increasing frequency of sudden-onset disasters will hasten environmental degradation and reduce resilience, rendering the distinction among drivers of cross-border migration "arbitrary or difficult to draw."[75] The United Nations predicts at least 4.4 million international migrants from Central America by 2040, not accounting for the conditional outflows brought on by sudden-onset disasters. Over this same period, the working-age population will expand by more than ten million, creating an even greater impetus for mass migration if local industries continue to underperform due to changing climate patterns.[76]

The reluctance of local governments to invest in adaptation, combined with an existing inability to rebound from natural disasters and the persistence of informal employment, suggests little change to future migration patterns. Thus, there is a high probability of internal displacement and international migration in the decades to come.

INTERSTATE TENSIONS

The countries of Central America have maintained nonhostile diplomatic relations in the modern era. Ideological and diplomatic disagreements have mostly taken a back-seat to the intergovernmental consensus that cooperation and integration are fundamental to resolving common challenges and becoming more economically competitive. In 1993, the region established the Central American Integration System to facilitate dispute resolution among its seven member states, promote democratic governance, reduce poverty and inequality, and harmonize economic policies. And in the 2010s, some Central American governments, the U.S. government, and the Inter-American Development Bank devised a joint strategy to address irregular migration by prioritizing economic growth and employment, developing the region's human capital, improving citizen security, and strengthening access to justice.

However, entrenched corruption and rising authoritarianism in Central America have increasingly stymied the ambitions of the last decade. In El Salvador, Guatemala, Honduras, and Nicaragua, national leaders have pursued tolerant relations with their counterparts not based on shared values but rather on their shared vulnerability to prosecution and conviction, undercutting their rhetorical commitment to inclusivity, human rights, and the rule of law. Nicaragua's Ortega administration is a most extreme example, providing safe haven for former presidents of El Salvador sought in their own country on corruption charges, all while systematically dismantling institutional checks and balances, the independent media, and civil society at home.

Costa Rica and Panama have led efforts to reinvigorate regional consensus on democracy via the Alliance for Development in Democracy, and Costa Rica's new President Rodrigo Chaves has opted for diplomacy instead of disengagement from the region's authoritarian leaders. However, growing frustration with government oppression in Nicaragua, which has contributed to migrant outflows, combined with the demographic strains induced by climate change, could soon spark a period of rising interstate tensions. Historically, southward Central American migration to the wealthier Costa Rica and Panama seldom sparked major discord. Yet Nicaraguans saw their numbers in Costa Rica rise by 44 percent between 2006 and 2020.[77] And the COVID-19 pandemic, an economic recession, and larger northbound migrant flows from Venezuela prompted a rise in hostile rhetoric and xenophobic policies directed at Nicaraguans.[78] The significant socio-economic divide between Costa Rica and Panama and the rest of Central America already fuels a sense of southern exceptionalism—one magnified during times of economic downturn. In a job-scarce and resource-competitive environment, Costa Rica and Panama could prove more resistant to accommodating and integrating new migrants.

Moreover, the entire Central American isthmus serves as a thoroughfare for South American, Caribbean, and extra-continental migrants en route to Mexico and the United States; some of these individuals are themselves fleeing the effects of climate change in their home countries. From 2014 to 2019, the number of African and Asian migrants transiting Panama's Darien, a densely forested and largely uninhabited area of jungle that connects Central America with South America, increased by 715 percent. A vast network of criminal organizations, taking advantage of government corruption and ineffectiveness, facilitates this unprecedented flow of migrants into the region and fuels predatory violence against migrants and regional residents.[79] If Central American authorities eventually decide to crack down on these trafficking networks and enforce borders, the resulting redirection of the migration flow could generate tensions with other governments along the transit routes that would stand to receive increased migration, including Colombia, Mexico, and the island nations of the Caribbean.

In fact, Mexico, not Central America, will likely face the greatest instability caused by climate-related migration, given its unique position between major source countries in Central America and the United States and as an international migration destination in its own right. The flow of illicit goods and undocumented people through Mexico, facilitated by regional trafficking networks, has contributed to the country's record-high homicide rates, and the Mexican government's enforcement of its northern and southern borders has created pockets of misery and insecurity where migrants concentrate in hopes of eventually making it to the United States.

Beyond the pressures introduced by human mobility, economic disparities brought on by employment shortages and access to energy could also aggravate interstate relations in the future. In Panama, droughts have led to water shortages that limit the amount of cargo weight that ships can transfer through the Panama Canal's locks, curbing the economic potential of the county's most important driver of growth and jeopardizing the country's long-standing reputation as a healthy market for international investors.[80] The challenges posed by climate change there could eventually put tens of thousands of well-paying jobs at risk if authorities fail to modernize the canal's infrastructure—even more so if Arctic shipping routes open as a result of climate change and compete with Panama's Caribbean-Pacific one. Further north, Guatemala enjoys a privileged position at Mexico's southern border, which reduces transaction costs for imported goods and makes the country a major exporter of electricity to the rest of Central America.[81] Depending on how exposed Central American supply chains and power grids become to international fluctuations in commodities prices, climate change could put Guatemala in a position to set commercial and energy policies that would benefit its own population at the expense of its poorer neighbors.

The same goes for water resources, as Guatemala, which boasts more than double the global average for freshwater availability per habitant, is an important exporter of water to its neighbors.[82] Likewise, interstate rivalry for shared resources—be they freshwater deposits along territorial borders or fishing waters along still-disputed maritime borders—could result in major diplomatic or legal disputes among the countries of Central America.[83] Guatemalan companies in recent years set up sand mining operations on Honduran rivers for the production of cement, advancing the process of desertification in Honduras.[84] The destruction of common habitats—such as the mangrove ecosystem of the Gulf of Fonseca that runs along the Salvadoran, Honduran, and Nicaraguan coast—by one country could have ramifications that transcend national borders and ultimately serve as a major source of regional friction.

In the absence of cooperative strategies for managing shared spaces, interstate tensions will be inevitable but, overall, unlikely to result in an armed confrontation. The region's armed forces have little interest and no recent experience in mounting and sustaining a military campaign against neighboring countries, and the stakes of resource competition, at least for 2040, are unlikely to reach such levels for which diplomatic resolutions are beyond reach. Even so, public officials are still apt to utilize resource constraints to rile nationalism when politically expedient, a prospect that is not without the risk of inter-community violence.

The most significant potential flashpoint is a long-standing Belize-Guatemala border dispute. Skirmishes in the contested area over fishing rights, wildlife poaching, and conservation efforts have persisted for years between Belizeans and Guatemalans.[85] As of 2022, after holding referendums in both countries, the case sits with the International Court of Justice for international arbitration. Regardless of any eventual ruling, politicians in both countries could exploit historically tense relations to rally their populations to defend claimed resources.

Looking out to 2040, climate change will undoubtedly contribute to interstate tensions among the countries of Central America. However, the likelihood that intraregional migration and resource competition erupt as conflict is lower, thanks to an outflow of people to wealthier economies and the tradition of managing disputes without involving security forces. Overall, interstate tensions related to climate change post a moderate probability of driving instability in Central America.

RECOMMENDATIONS

Climate-induced instability is already taking place, especially as it relates to human mobility, but improving the lives of Central Americans and ensuring that climate change does not result in societal collapse are achievable. To this end, in the past decade the governments of Central America have all published thorough national adaptation plans to reduce climate change's environmental and human costs. However, modest national investments to this end have failed to keep pace with the needs of affected communities, as evidenced by recent progress reports submitted to the UN Framework Convention on Climate Change.[86] Politically influential agribusiness associations have also proved reluctant to embrace—let alone lead—a green transition in the countryside, instead lobbying authorities to prevent regulations that require sustainable practices. Furthermore, the COVID-19 pandemic and the associated economic recession left government institutions overextended and cash-strapped, derailing governmental capacity to meet targets.

Generating additional challenges, the geopolitical shifts underway in the region do not bode well for the needed climate-focused transformation. The growing development needs are occurring at a time when U.S.-Central American relations are more strained than at any point since the 1990s, reducing the leverage of the region's biggest benefactor to elicit cooperation from the many regional officials whom the U.S. government has sanctioned over malfeasance and corruption. Similarly, the devastation of Eta and Iota followed on the heels of major funding cuts for environmental initiatives and the Green Climate Fund by the Donald Trump administration, underscoring susceptibility of the region's resilience strategies to changing political winds in donor countries.[87] And as Central American governments look for investors elsewhere, China is an eager partner, expanding its economic footprint on the isthmus with little concern for climate sustainability.[88] Moreover, across Latin America, governments are increasingly pursuing policies of nonalignment in an era of multipolar competition—at once denouncing Russia's invasion of Ukraine but refusing to join Western sanctions against Moscow in a bid to retain access to Russian agricultural and energy resources.[89]

Instability due to climate change in Central America is not inevitable. Despite economic, political, and diplomatic hurdles, Central America's neighbors, especially the United States and Mexico, can and should do more. The solution lies in working with Central American administrations where authorities can find common cause, while leveraging ties to civil society, the private sector, and multilateral organizations to usher in changes where governments cannot.

RECOMMENDATIONS FOR CENTRAL AMERICA

Improve the analytical capacity of governments to diagnose the problem. El Salvador, Guatemala, Honduras, and Nicaragua possess limited tools to monitor, model, and evaluate the effects of climate change in their national territories, especially in more remote areas of the country where weather substations do not exist. Without a clear notion of the expected intensity and scope of the future climate crisis, government-led interventions will remain haphazard and possibly misguided. Small-scale research initiatives—be it an aquarium to study reef decay or a food insecurity institute at a local university—demonstrate promise for local problem solving. Regional governments should build on and subsidize such initiatives and prioritize data collection to diagnose and support adaptation more effectively. More granular meteorological data could inform government communications to the public about when to plant and harvest crops to minimize crop failure and boost productivity. Costa Rica and Panama offer compelling regional examples of how greater governance and investment in climate analysis can reduce regional vulnerability. The experiences of those countries should inform the strategies of their northern neighbors.

Invest in hazard-monitoring systems and citizen training to prevent extreme weather events from becoming humanitarian disasters. Climate events develop into humanitarian disasters because of human unpreparedness. Regional governments should invest in risk-monitoring and detection systems for endemic climate events such as forest fires and flooding. Despite improvements in hurricane, tsunami, and earthquake early-warning systems in Central America, only 36 percent of affected Hondurans had access to early-warning information during Eta and Iota.[90] And even many individuals who did receive alerts in high-risk areas refused to relocate because of distrust in authorities and unfamiliarity with disaster-prevention approaches.[91] First, regional security forces should receive specialized training in first responder protocols, the appropriate use of force, and gender and cultural considerations relevant to humanitarian assistance responsibilities. Second, community-based training on risk reduction and climate adaptation should involve authorities at all levels of government, nongovernmental organizations, the private sector, and local universities and schools. These interventions would help build the awareness, skills, and trust needed to survive future climate events.

Fund adaptation nationally but devise adaptation plans locally.
National governments need to invigorate existing adaptation plans but should do so in ways that encourage local participation and account for local preferences. Civil society organizations, including agricultural cooperatives and communal forest associations, possess the local knowledge to be useful allies. Some pilot interventions are already bearing results. In Honduras, building local reserve capacity within energy grids through solar, wind, and microhydraulic technology has enabled more isolated communities to sustain their activities when weather events disconnect them.[92] The distribution of eco-friendly cookstoves (*ecofogones*) has also reduced community emissions and the incidence of forest fires. In Guatemala, monoculture communities that have diversified their agricultural output and introduced more drought-resistant crop varieties have managed to subsist despite variation in the *canícula*.[93]

Throughout the region, some smallholders are returning to more sustainable agricultural techniques, known as agroecology. Yet because these methods are labor intensive and produce a lower yield in the near term, governments should incentivize a wholesale transition by providing technical assistance and subsidies to participating communities. The last twenty years witnessed an overreliance on public water systems and imported commercial products to boost crop yield, ironically depleting the soil of naturally occurring nutrients. But Central American farmers historically accumulated water during the rainy season to irrigate crops during drought, and they used organic and locally available materials to fertilize and protect their crops from pests. Silvopasture, or the deliberate integration of trees and grazing livestock farms, was implemented by the Mayans to increase water availability while supporting soil conservation and biodiversity growth. These traditional agricultural practices should be at the core of rural climate resilience.

Revamp laws in ways that account for the permanence of a climate crisis. Most regional governments are not proactive when it comes to climate events. Because of the urgency of reconstruction after a climate event, government decision-making does not sufficiently incorporate resilience strategies. With the infusion of new climate data into decision-making, authorities should update building codes and zoning surveys in ways that prioritize climate resilience to prevent tragedy before weather events strike. This step is especially necessary as cities become more crowded and city dwellers place a growing strain on nationwide utilities and public services provision.

To keep pace with expanding demand, authorities should also raise national budgets and, thus, taxes to fund resilience-related activities. A tax on the tourism industry, for instance, could help fill resource gaps. As Costa Rica powerfully demonstrates, sustainable tourism represents a major opportunity for Central America—prior to the COVID-19 pandemic, the region already played host to some eleven million tourists per year.[94] Instead of offering value-added tax (VAT) refunds for foreign visitors, Central American governments should consider "green taxes" or "adaptation credits" that tap into tourists' growing sense of individual social responsibility and direct collected revenues toward advancing carbon neutrality and funding national climate adaptation plans.

RECOMMENDATIONS FOR THE UNITED STATES, MEXICO, AND OTHER INDUSTRIALIZED NATIONS

Implement legal reforms and expand institutional budgets to accommodate increased asylum and refugee petitions, and expand on temporary worker programs to meet labor needs. Even though people displaced by climate change are not protected under the 1951 Refugee Convention, the United States and Mexico are already adapting to increased demand for protection by enforcing mechanisms that prohibit deportation to high-risk countries, such as humanitarian visas and temporary protected status.[95] However, Mexican cities such as Tapachula and Tijuana habitually play host to tens of thousands of refugees and migrants, many of whom live on the streets; this scenario demonstrates that the capacity to absorb and integrate migrants does not meet current demand, let alone that of the future. As the principal destination countries for Central American migrants and asylum seekers, the United States and Mexico need larger, better staffed, and better resourced border agencies.

As worker shortages in the United States limit productivity in agriculture and services, the U.S. government should also prioritize the enlargement of H-2A and H-2B nonimmigrant visas for temporary laborers from priority countries in Central America. The present "closed-door" policies, in fact, raise the stakes for Central Americans in ways that encourage migration instead of short-term relocation or climate-change adaptation. Many potential migrants would forgo the dangerous trek northward if they had assurances of work and opportunities to visit loved ones under guest worker programs.

Build on hemispheric migrant and refugee resettlement accords to distribute humanitarian obligations more equitably. The United States and Mexico should stop treating migration as a perpetual national security threat that requires a contingent military response at the border and, instead, respond to rising human mobility through humane and sustainable processes. To reduce the administrative and financial strain on any one country in response to a global challenge, regional governments should share the responsibility to integrate migrants into their countries. At the June 2022 Summit of the Americas, twenty governments in the Western Hemisphere, with Spain as an observer, signed the "Los Angeles Declaration," committing to strengthening protection systems for migrants, expanding their access to legal pathways for work, and stabilizing host countries.

At a time when regional economies have not fully recovered to pre-pandemic levels, the United States, Canada, Mexico, and other wealthier countries should underwrite in-region refugee resettlement initiatives that relocate applicants to a third country capable of absorbing them.[96] Doing so would help reduce long processing times and substantial case backlogs at the U.S. southwestern border, diminishing the dangers that many candidates confront while awaiting a determination of status.[97]

Enhance the capacity of civilian agencies and regional security forces to respond to disasters, prioritizing intraregional cooperation. Central American civilian disaster preparedness agencies lack funding, sufficient staff, and response capabilities.[98] As a result, they tend to rely on regional militaries for disaster response, given their superior logistical capacity and ability to mobilize transportation resources rapidly. The Departments of State and Defense should prioritize humanitarian assistance and disaster response capabilities through security assistance. For their part, the U.S. Department of Homeland Security's Federal Emergency Management Agency (FEMA) and USAID should work with regional disaster response coordinators to review protocols and strategize improved civil-military coordination and provide more robust funding for regional counterparts.

In addition, the U.S. and Mexican governments should expand regional training that encourages interoperability among Central American responders so that, for instance, Guatemalan forces can bring to bear their capabilities in Honduras and vice versa when disaster strikes. To this end, the Central American Coordination Center for the Prevention of Natural Disasters (CEPREDENAC) should be a high-priority beneficiary for donors, as it has the expertise and vision to carry out regionally harmonized responses to climate events but often lacks adequate resources.

Help retool Central American economies to generate employment and prioritize climate resilience through development assistance. Agriculture will continue to be an important driver of growth in Central America, but environmental degradation and the reduction of arable land will require other industries to absorb part of the rural workforce. To meet future labor needs, Central America will need to attract greater private investment in industrial activities. Vice President Kamala Harris's "Call to Action for Northern Central America" is an important first step in generating new business and employment opportunities, but Central America's manufacturing potential remains untapped; nearshoring, or the relocation of U.S. industrial operations to the Americas, is an attractive option for staving off economic anxiety.

Even with these kinds of investments, rural populations will still require support. At present, U.S. development assistance to agriculture accounts for a relatively small portion of total U.S. foreign assistance to Central America, but climate-smart agriculture requires up-front investments that are often unfeasible for smallholder farmers.[99] The U.S. Development Finance Corporation should enlarge financing and insurance for renewables and conservation projects, making green technology more affordable to low-income countries. The U.S. Agency for International Development should expand funding for the Central American countryside, prioritizing technical assistance for sustainable agriculture and infrastructure to help communities withstand climate events.

Overall, the U.S. government and like-minded donors such as the European Union and regional development banks should improve coordination to avoid the duplication of efforts, and the world's wealthiest governments, which also represent the globe's top carbon emitters, should mobilize greater resources to adaptation efforts in the low-income countries in Central America. In Nicaragua, where the U.S. government is reluctant to administer foreign assistance due to sanctions against the Ortega administration, multilateral lenders and partner countries that retain a development presence in Nicaragua should prioritize climate-focused conditionality in their dealings with Nicaraguan authorities.

RECOMMENDATIONS FOR MULTILATERAL ORGANIZATIONS AND THE PRIVATE SECTOR

Support asylum processing and migrant resettlement by providing reliable information to potential applicants and by guiding national procedures to ensure fairness and competence. As governments throughout the Western Hemisphere make a renewed effort at equitable migrant and refugee resettlement, civil society and organizations such as the UN High Commissioner for Refugees and the International Organization for Migration are well positioned to collect information from candidates and prioritize cases for consideration by national authorities in destination countries. Their inputs should inform government-orchestrated migration across borders. To streamline the coordination of such efforts, the United Nations should improve transient housing for displaced people by financing the construction of new facilities in source countries and destination countries alike. This move could help reduce the incidence of predatory violence against migrants and refugees who are often huddled into informal settlements while waiting for access to border crossings. It would also signal a recognition of the permanence of the human mobility challenge in the Americas, something regional governments have long been reluctant to acknowledge.

Cancel some regional debt in exchange for local conservation investments and finance adaptation. Governments in Central America suffer from a high ratio of debt to gross domestic product (GDP)—more than 50 percent in El Salvador, Costa Rica, Honduras,

Nicaragua, and Panama.[100] The multilateral lending organizations that hold much of this debt, such as the Inter-American Development Bank and the International Monetary Fund, should forgive some of it, contingent on national investments in environmental conservation. The Spanish government has delivered some debt relief for reforestation projects in protected biospheres in Honduras, providing a template for "debt-for-nature swaps." Freeing up budgets by reducing annual debt service would facilitate national buy-in to protect and revitalize at-risk ecosystems such as cloud forests and coral reefs. Conservation investments would be especially important in places where environmental protection translates into major economic benefits such as the Panama Canal, which depends on heavily forested areas to produce the freshwater necessary for the proper functioning of the canal's locks. Central America's ecological wealth, including oxygen repositories in heavily forested areas, present significant opportunities for local economies and global decarbonization.

Likewise, lenders to the region should ensure any new loans advance climate sustainability goals. The Central American Bank for Economic Integration has begun important work in this realm, delivering more than 41 percent of its funding to green projects, but carbon footprint reduction has been the foremost focus, even though Central America contributes so little to global carbon emissions.[101] Reorienting investments to mitigate climate change while also advancing the region's adaptive needs is a necessary step.

Establish national or regional trusts using private sector contributions to subsidize coping strategies and adaptation measures. Effective tax rates in Central America are significantly below the Latin American average, denying governments the flexibility to redirect existing revenues to subsidize a green transition, sustainable infrastructure, and local adaptation strategies. However, regional businesses resist paying higher taxes in part due to pervasive public corruption. Elsewhere in Latin America, governments have applied taxes on bank transactions or payrolls with the consent of business associations for clearly defined public goods, such as crime prevention, on the condition that the private sector have oversight in the administration of monies and implementation of strategies.[102] Such a mechanism could help address climate change fallout, too. Establishing national or even regional trusts, administered by nongovernmental or multilateral organizations, that permit Central American corporations to make contributions while exerting control over how their pooled resources are spent could help the region address aspects of the climate crisis. For instance, existing government-run agricultural insurance programs that provide economic coverage to small producers for crop loss are limited in scope, poorly administered, and entail high premiums. A public-private trust built around a continuous revenue stream, on the other hand, could offer low-rate financing for coping and adaptation alike, while assuring greater access to and transparency and sustainability of assistance programs.

CONCLUSION

Looking ahead to 2040, current climate trends are set to intensify, accelerating environmental degradation, food and energy insecurity, urbanization, and societal violence. Those conditions, against a backdrop of inequality and corruption, will exacerbate living conditions for Central Americans, many of whom will seek opportunities to live outside of their communities and often outside of their countries due to internal disorder fueled by climate change. Increased human mobility and heightened resource competition will rile tensions among countries in the region, while fomenting disorder in places such as Mexico and at the U.S. southwestern border. Although these stressors are unlikely to generate large-scale conflict within or between states, their effects will be just as destabilizing. After all, regional indicators of violence and displacement have been higher in peacetime than ever before, including when the region was convulsed in civil wars.

To stave off climate-induced instability in Central America, national governments and regional and international organizations all have a role to play to develop both immediate crisis response and long-term instability mitigation. Indeed, a period of great migration in the Americas has already commenced, owing in part to the compounding effects of climate change on long-standing regional challenges, and El Salvador, Guatemala, Honduras, and Nicaragua represent today's crisis epicenter. But the tale of Central America in the twenty-first century is not fated to be one of persistent tragedy. With greater investments in government capacity, community adaptation, and international cooperation, Central Americans can rewrite their story, instead, as one of resilience and even hope.

ENDNOTES

1. D'vera Cohn, Jeffrey S. Passel, and Ana Gonzalez-Barrera, "Rise in U.S. Immigrants From El Salvador, Guatemala and Honduras Outpaces Growth From Elsewhere," Pew Research Center, December 7, 2017, https://www.pewresearch.org/hispanic/2017/12/07/rise-in-u-s-immigrants-from-el-salvador-guatemala-and-honduras-outpaces-growth-from-elsewhere; "Southwest Land Border Encounters," U.S. Customs and Border Protection, June 15, 2022, https://www.cbp.gov/newsroom/stats/southwest-land-border-encounters; and "Boletín Mensual de Estadísitcas Migratorias," Secretaría de Gobernación, May 2022, http://www.portales.segob.gob.mx/es/PoliticaMigratoria/Boletines_Estadisticos.

2. "Hunger in Central America Skyrockets, U.N. Agency Says," Reuters, February 23, 2021, https://www.reuters.com/article/us-central-america-hunger-idUSKBN2AO03C.

3. Sönke Kreft, David Eckstein, and Inga Melchior, "Global Climate Risk Index 2017," Germanwatch, November 2016, https://www.germanwatch.org/en/12978.

4. "Rankings—2019," University of Notre Dame, Notre Dame Global Adaptation Initiative, https://gain.nd.edu/our-work/country-index/rankings.

5. Hannah Ritchie, Max Roser, and Pablo Rosado, "CO_2 and Greenhouse Gas Emissions," Our World in Data, August 2020, https://ourworldindata.org/co2-emissions.

6. "What Is Human Security?," Inter-American Institute of Human Rights, Human Security in Latin America, 2010, https://www.iidh.ed.cr/multic/default_12.aspx?contenidoid=ea75e2b1-9265-4296-9d8c-3391de83fb42&Portal=IIDHSeguridadEN; and Yuriv Vayskin, Claire Lackerby, and Steven McMullen, "The Soccer War," Duke University, Soccer Politics, 2009, https://sites.duke.edu/wcwp/research-projects/the-soccer-war.

7. Caitlin E. Werrell and Francesco Femia, "Climate Change as Threat Multiplier: Understanding the Broader Nature of the Risk," Center for Climate and Security, February 12, 2014, https://climateandsecurity.org/wp-content/uploads/2012/04/climate-change-as-threat-multiplier_understanding-the-broader-nature-of-the-risk_briefer-252.pdf.

8. "FY 2016. Congressional Budget Justification - Foreign Assistance," Department of State, February 2, 2015, https://www.usaid.gov/sites/default/files/documents/9276/FY16CBJStateFORP.pdf.

9. Kenneth Seligson, "Misreading the Story of Climate Change and the Maya," The Conversation, May 20, 2019, http://theconversation.com/misreading-the-story-of-climate-change-and-the-maya-113829.

10. Lisa Viscidi and M.K. Vereen, "Climate Threats in the Northern Triangle: How the United States Can Support Community Resilience," Inter-American Dialogue, February 2022, https://www.thedialogue.org/analysis/climate-threats-in-the-northern-triangle-how-the-united-states-can-support-community-resilience.

11. Steven M. Whitfield, Karen R. Lips, and Maureen A. Donnelly, "Amphibian Decline and Conservation in Central America," American Society of Ichthyologists and Herpetologists, May 18, 2016, https://meridian.allenpress.com/copeia/article-abstract/104/2/351/196438/Amphibian-Decline-and-Conservation-in-Central?redirectedFrom=fulltext.

12. Cervantes Martínez et al., "Historical Bark Beetle Outbreaks in Mexico, Guatemala, and Honduras (1985–2015) and Their Relationship With Droughts," Revista Chapingo Serie Ciencias Forestales y del Ambiente 25, no. 2 (August 2019): 269–90, https://revistas.chapingo.mx/forestales/?section=articles&subsec=issues&numero=271&articulo=2582.

13. Avelino Jacques, "The Coffee Rust Crisis in Central America," American Phyto-pathological Society, March 2016, https://agritrop.cirad.fr/580046.

14. Ana Ríos (senior specialist, Inter-American Development Bank), in interview with the author, Tegucigalpa, Honduras, May 2, 2022.

15. "Climate Change in Central America: Potential Impacts and Public Policy Options," Economic Commission for Latin America and the Caribbean, August 2018, https://www.cepal.org/en/publications/39150-climate-change-central-america-potential-impacts-and-public-policy-options; and "A Tiny Endangered Country," Revista Envío, January 1998, https://www.envio.org.ni/articulo/1315.

16. Tony Borsak (director, Tela Marine Research Center), in interview with the author, Tela, Honduras, May 6, 2022. As of early 2022, long-spined sea urchins in the Caribbean, which are critical to reef health, are facing rapid and widespread mortality. Likewise, the past decade has witnessed pervasive sponge orange band disease and stony coral tissue loss disease, affecting overall marine stocks of sea sponges and coral.

17. Eugenia Recio et al., "Central America Mangroves, Tenure, and REDD+ Assessment," USAID, January 2016, https://www.land-links.org/wp-content/uploads/2018/03/USAID_Land_Tenure_TGCC_Central_America_Mangroves_REDD_Assessment_Tenure.pdf.

18. "Climate Change Risk Profile: Honduras," USAID, March 2017, https://pdf.usaid.gov/pdf_docs/PA00MVPV.pdf.

19. Yolanda González (director of research, Team for Reflection, Research, and Communications, Radio Progreso), in interview with the author, El Progreso, Honduras, May 6, 2022.

20. "Climate Change in Central America: Potential Impacts and Public Policy Options," Economic Commission for Latin America and the Caribbean, August 2018, https://www.cepal.org/en/publications/39150-climate-change-central-america-potential-impacts-and-public-policy-options.

21. "Central America: Meet People's Needs and Tackle Root Causes of Migration, Says Report," World Food Programme, November 23, 2021, https://www.wfp.org/stories

/central-america-meet-peoples-needs-and-tackle-root-causes-migration-says-report; and World Food Programme (@WFP), 2021, "The number of hungry people across Central America has nearly quadrupled over 2 years," Twitter, April 18, 2021, https:// twitter.com/WFP/status/1383837086273327109.

22. "Regional Overview of Food Security and Nutrition in Latin America and the Caribbean 2021: Facts and Figures," Food and Agriculture Organization of the United Nations, November 30, 2021, https://iris.paho.org/handle/10665.2/55213.

23. "Guatemala: Nutrition Profile," USAID, December, 2021, https://www.usaid.gov/sites /default/files/documents/Copy_of_Guatemala-Nutrition-Profile_1.pdf.

24. "Malnutrition Among Children in Latin America and the Caribbean," Economic Commission for Latin America and the Caribbean, April 2, 2018, https://www.cepal.org/en /insights/malnutrition-among-children-latin-america-and-caribbean.

25. Melissa A. Adelman and Miguel Székely, "An Overview of School Dropout in Central America: Unresolved Issues and New Challenges for Education Progress," *European Journal of Educational Research* 6, no. 3 (July 2017): 235–59, https://eric.ed.gov /?id=EJ1149727.

26. "Honduras Overview: Development news, research, data," The World Bank, April 25, 2022, https://www.worldbank.org/en/country/honduras/overview.

27. "Climate Change Risk Profile: Honduras."

28. "Climate Change Risk Profile: Guatemala," USAID, April 2017, https://www.climatelinks .org/resources/climate-risk-profile-guatemala.

29. Alex Guerra (director, Private Institute for Climate Change Research), in interview with the author, Esquintla, Guatemala, January 26, 2022.

30. "Data and Statistics: Agricultural Development," Economic Commission for Latin America and the Caribbean, 2017, https://www.cepal.org/en/datos-y-estadisticas -desarrollo-agricola.

31. Diana Feliciano and Alejandra Sobenes, "Stakeholders' Perceptions of Factors Influencing Climate Change Risk in a Central America Hotspot," *Regional Environmental Change*, February 22, 2022, https://link.springer.com/content/pdf/10.1007/s10113-022-01885-4.pdf.

32. Carrie Kahn, "Rust Devastates Guatemala's Prime Coffee Crop and Its Farmers," NPR, July 28, 2014, https://www.npr.org/sections/thesalt/2014/07/28/335293974/rust-devastates -guatemalas-prime-coffee-crop-and-its-farmers.

33. "Honduras Overview: Development News, Research, Data," World Bank, April 25, 2022, https://www.worldbank.org/en/country/honduras/overview.

34. "Social Panorama of Latin America 2021," Economic Commission for Latin America and the Caribbean, January 2022, https://www.cepal.org/en/publications/47719-social -panorama-latin-america-2021.

35. "Country Profile: Guatemala," USAID, Land Links, 2010, https://www.land-links.org /country-profile/guatemala.

36. "Climate Change in Central America: Potential Impacts and Public Policy Options," Economic Commission for Latin America and the Caribbean, August 2018, https://www

.cepal.org/en/publications/39150-climate-change-central-america-potential-impacts
-and-public-policy-options.

37. "Climate Change in Central America: Potential Impacts and Public Policy Options."

38. Cristina Enache, "OECD Report: Tax Revenue as a Percent of GDP in Latin American and Caribbean Countries Is Below the OECD Average," Tax Foundation, April 28, 2021, https://taxfoundation.org/latin-american-tax-revenue-caribbean-tax-revenue; and "Guatemala's Public Spending: Worst in the World?," Entremundos, no date is provided, https://www.entremundos.org/revista/economy/guate-in-graphs/guatemalas-public-spending-worst-in-the-world/?lang=en.

39. Pablo Bachelet, "How Does Trust Impact Your Quality of Life?," Inter-American Development Bank, accessed August 8, 2022, https://www.iadb.org/en/improvinglives/how-does-trust-impact-your-quality-life.

40. Reese Erlich, "Controversy Runs Deep in Nicaragua's Canal Plan," Al Jazeera, February 24, 2015, http://america.aljazeera.com/opinions/2015/2/nicaragua-launches-worlds-largest-infrastructure-project.html#:~:text=Under%20the%20new%20terms%2C%20HKND,sellout%20of%20the%20country's%20sovereignty.

41. Anne Tittor, "Conflicts About Nicaragua's Interoceanic Canal Project: Framing, Counter-framing and Government Strategies," *Cahiers des Amériques Latines* 87(2018): 117–40, https://journals.openedition.org/cal/8561.

42. Nicaraguan migrants, interview with the author, Tapachula, Mexico, January 25, 2022.

43. Yolanda González (director of research, Team for Reflection, Research, and Communications, Radio Progreso), in interview with the author, El Progreso, Honduras, May 6, 2022.

44. Nina Lakhani, "Two More Honduran Land Rights Activists Killed in Ongoing Violence," *The Guardian*, October 19, 2016. https://www.theguardian.com/world/2016/oct/19/honduras-land-rights-activists-killed-unified-peasant-movement.

45. "Global Witness Reports 227 Land and Environmental Activists Murdered in a Single Year, the Worst Figure on Record," Global Witness, September 13, 2021, https://www.globalwitness.org/en/press-releases/global-witness-reports-227-land-and-environmental-activists-murdered-single-year-worst-figure-record.

46. Lisa Viscidi and M.K. Vereen, "Climate Threats in the Northern Triangle: How the United States Can Support Community Resilience," Inter-American Dialogue, February 2022, https://www.thedialogue.org/analysis/climate-threats-in-the-northern-triangle-how-the-united-states-can-support-community-resilience.

47. "10 cosas que debes saber del caso Ciudad del Ángel," *La Prensa*, April 12, 2020, https://www.laprensa.hn/fotogalerias/honduras/10-cosas-que-debes-saber-del-caso-ciudad-del-angel-GDLP1427098.

48. Yolanda González (director, Research Team for Reflection, Research, and Communications, Radio Progreso), in interview with the author, El Progreso, Honduras, May 6, 2022; and Josué Zelaya (director, Casa Alianza Regional Office), in interview with the author, San Pedro Sula, Honduras, May 9, 2022.

49. Emilliano Rodríguez Mega, "Cocaine Trafficking Is Destroying Central America's Forests," *Science*, June 16, 2017, https://www.science.org/content/article/cocaine -trafficking-destroying-central-america-s-forests.

50. Jeff Ernst, "Mountain Labs Turn Honduras From Cocaine Way Station Into Producer," *The Guardian*, May 24, 2022, https://www.theguardian.com/world/2022/may/24/honduras -cocaine-production-narcotics-central-america.

51. Claudia Herrera Melgar (executive secretary, Central American Coordination Center for the Prevention of Natural Disasters), in interview with the author, Guatemala City, Guatemala, January 27, 2022; and "Countries by Population Density 2022," World Population Review, https://worldpopulationreview.com/country-rankings/countries -by-density.

52. "World Population Prospects—2019," United Nations, Department of Economic and Social Affairs, https://population.un.org/wpp/DataQuery.

53. Felix Baquedano et al., "International Food Security Assessment, 2021–31 (GFA-32)," U.S. Department of Agriculture, Economic Research Service, July 2021, https://www .ers.usda.gov/webdocs/outlooks/101733/gfa-32.pdf?v=4090. El Salvador is the one country in the region where population growth rates are expected to decline due to emigration, largely to the United States.

54. "High Food and Commodity Prices Drive Food Insecurity at the Start of the Lean Season," Famine Early Warning System, May 2022, https://fews.net/central-america -and-caribbean/key-message-update/may-2022.

55. Felix Baquedano et al., "International Food Security Assessment, 2021–31 (GFA-32)."

56. "Climate Change Risk Profile: Guatemala." Ana Ríos (senior specialist, Inter-American Development Bank), in interview with the author, Tegucigalpa, Honduras, May 2, 2022. Presently at least one million people in Honduras are employed in the coffee industry, and some 20 percent of the country's exports are related to coffee.

57. "Climate Refugees—Spotlight: The Northern Triangle (Guatemala, Honduras and El Salvador)," Othering & Belonging Institute, accessed August 9, 2022, https://belonging .berkeley.edu/climate-refugees.

58. Sofia Méndez (environmental compliance officer, USAID Honduras), in interview with the author, Tegucigalpa, Honduras, May 3, 2022.

59. "Climate Impacts Latin American Hydropower," International Energy Agency, January 2021, https://www.iea.org/reports/climate-impacts-on-latin-american-hydropower.

60. "Mexico, the Caribbean, and Central America: The Impact of Climate Change to 2030," National Intelligence Council, December 2009, https://www.dni.gov/files/documents /climate2030_MexicoCaribCentralAm.pdf.

61. "The Slow Onset Effects of Climate Change and Human Rights Protection for Cross-Border Migrants," Office of the United Nations High Commissioner for Human Rights (OHCHR), March 22, 2018, https://disasterdisplacement.org/portfolio-item /slow-onset.

62. "Food Security and Emigration: Why People Flee and the Impact on Family Members Left Behind in El Salvador, Guatemala, and Honduras," United Nations World Food Programme, August 2017, https://docs.wfp.org/api/documents/WFP-0000019629/download.

63. María Augustin et al., "Central America Urbanization Review: Making Cities Work for Central America," World Bank Group, March 15, 2017, https://openknowledge .worldbank.org/handle/10986/26271.

64. Gabriela Bulnes (professor of nutrition and diet, National Autonomous University of Honduras), Comayagua, Honduras, May 4, 2022.

65. "Population Living in Slums (% of Urban Population). Latin America & Caribbean—2018," World Bank Group, accessed August 9, 2022, https://data.worldbank.org /indicator/EN.POP.SLUM.UR.ZS?locations=ZJ.

66. Russel King, Ronald Skeldon, and Julie Vullnetari, "Internal and International Migration: Bridging the Theoretical Divide," University of Sussex, Sussex Centre for Migration Research, December 2018, https://www.researchgate.net/publication/238714010_Internal _and_International_Migration_Bridging_the_Theoretical_Divide.

67. Dara Lind, "The 2014 Central American Migrant Crisis," Vox, October 10, 2014, https:// www.vox.com/2014/10/10/18088638/child-migrant-crisis-unaccompanied-alien-children -rio-grande-valley-obama-immigration.

68. Jeanne Batalova and Erin Babich, "Central American Immigrants in the United States," Migration Policy Institute, August 11, 2021, https://www.migrationpolicy.org/article /dominican-immigrants-united-states-2021.

69. Catherine E. Shoichet, "Central American Migrants Paid $2.2 Billion Trying to Reach the US," CNN, November 24, 2021, https://www.cnn.com/2021/11/24/us/central -american-migration-costs/index.html.

70. Alfredo Sánchez-Castañeda, "Informal Employment in Mexico and Central America: A Complex Phenomenon," *Revue de droit comparé du travail et de la sécurité sociale* 4 (2017): 96–109, https://journals.openedition.org/rdctss/2246.

71. Betilde Muñoz-Pogossian and Diego Chaves-González, "Environmental Explanations of Central American Migration: Challenges and Policy Recommendations," Florida International University, August 2021, https://digitalcommons.fiu.edu/cgi/viewcontent .cgi?article=1038&context=jgi_research.

72. Ana Ríos (senior specialist, Inter-American Development Bank), in interview with the author, Tegucigalpa, Honduras, May 2, 2022.

73. Sarah Bermeo and David Leblang, "Climate, Violence, and Honduran Migration to the United States," Brookings Institution, April 1, 2021, https://www.brookings.edu /blog/future-development/2021/04/01/climate-violence-and-honduran-migration-to -the-united-states.

74. USAID official, interview with the author, Guatemala City, Guatemala, January 27, 2022.

75. "The Slow Onset Effects of Climate Change and Human Rights Protection for Cross-Border Migrants," OHCHR, Platform on Disaster Displacement, March 22, 2018, https://disasterdisplacement.org/portfolio-item/slow-onset.

76. "World Population Prospects—2019," United Nations Department of Economic and Social Affairs, https://population.un.org/wpp/DataQuery/.

77. "Informes Estadísticos Anuales 2021," Dirección General de Migración y Extranjería, Gobierno de Costa Rica, accessed August 10, 2022, https://www.migracion.go.cr/Paginas/Centro%20de%20Documentaci%c3%b3n/Estad%c3%adsticas.aspx.

78. Javier Argueda, "Borders, Commerce, and COVID-19: The Tense Relations Between Costa Rica and Nicaragua," Buffett Institute for Global Affairs, Global Learning Office, accessed August 10, 2022, https://www.northwestern.edu/abroad/about/news/borders,-commerce,-and-covid-19-the-tense-relations-between-costa-rica-and-nicaragua.html; Vladmir Vásquez, "Xenophobia, the Second Pandemic to Spread in Costa Rica," *Voice of Guanacaste*, March 24, 2022, https://vozdeguanacaste.com/en/xenophobia-the-second-pandemic-to-spread-in-costa-rica; and "La xenophobia se incuba en el Congreso de Panamá," *El Economista*, July 17, 2019, https://www.eleconomista.com.mx/internacionales/La-xenofobia-se-incuba-en-el-Congreso-de-Panama-20190717-0133.html.

79. "Migration Data in Central America—2020," Migration Data Portal, https://www.migrationdataportal.org/regional-data-overview/migration-data-central-america.

80. Walt Bogdanich, Jacqueline Williams, and Ana Graciela Mendez, "The New Panama Canal: A Risky Bet," *New York Times*, June 22, 2016, https://www.nytimes.com/interactive/2016/06/22/world/americas/panama-canal.html.

81. "Guatemala Eyeing Bilateral Deals with Regional Power Market Pullout," BNAmericas, July 19, 2021, https://www.bnamericas.com/en/news/guatemala-eyeing-bilateral-deals-with-regional-power-market-pullout.

82. Hilda Turcio, "El mercado del agua y el saneamiento en Guatemala 2020," Oficina Económica y Comercial de la Embajada de España en Guatemala, October 14, 2020, https://www.icex.es/icex/es/navegacion-principal/todos-nuestros-servicios/informacion-de-mercados/paises/navegacion-principal/el-mercado/estudios-informes/DOC2020865682.html?idPais=GT.

83. Terance R. Lee, "The Management of Shared Water Resources in Latin America," *Natural Resources Journal* 35 (1995): 541–53, https://archivo.cepal.org/pdfs/Waterguide/05_lee_latin.pdf.

84. Gabriela Bulnes (professor of nutrition and diet, National Autonomous University of Honduras), in interview with the author, Comayagua, Honduras, May 4, 2022.

85. Arlenie Perez, Chin-Ta Chuang, and Farok Afero, "Belize-Guatemala Territorial Dispute and its Implications for Conservation," *Tropical Conservation Science* 2, no. 1 (2009) 11–24, https://journals.sagepub.com/doi/full/10.1177/194008290900200104.

86. "National Communication Submissions from Non-Annex I Parties," UN Framework Convention on Climate Change, accessed August 10, 2022, https://unfccc.int/non-annex-I-NCs.

87. Lisa Viscidi and M.K. Vereen, "Climate Threats in the Northern Triangle: How the United States Can Support Community Resilience," Inter-American Dialogue, February 2022, https://www.thedialogue.org/analysis/climate-threats-in-the-northern-triangle-how-the-united-states-can-support-community-resilience.

88. Shannon O'Neil, "China's Green Investments Won't Undo Its Environmental Damage to Latin America," *Latin America's Moment* blog, Council on Foreign Relations, April 25,

2019, https://www.cfr.org/blog/chinas-green-investments-wont-undo-its-environmental-damage-latin-america.

89. Brian Winter, "On Fire: Europe's Woes Reverberate in Latin America," *Americas Quarterly*, August 25, 2022, https://www.americasquarterly.org/article/on-fire-europes-woes-reverberate-in-latin-america.

90. Ana Ríos (senior specialist at the Inter-American Development Bank), in interview with the author, Tegucigalpa, Honduras, May 2, 2022.

91. Laura Fajardo Cabus (director of social development, National Foundation for Honduran Development), in interview with the author, San Pedro Sula, Honduras, May 9, 2022.

92. Alex Maffeis (Honduras country manager, RE.TE.ONG), in interview with the author, Tegucigalpa, Honduras, May 2, 2022.

93. Alex Guerra (director, Private Institute for Climate Change Research), in interview with the author, Esquintla, Guatemala, January 26, 2022.

94. Ana M. López, "International Tourism in Central America—Statistics and Facts," Statista, May 24, 2022, https://www.statista.com/topics/9273/international-tourism-in-central-america.

95. Andrés Ramírez (director, Mexican Commission for Refugee Assistance), in interview with the author, Mexico City, Mexico, January 24, 2022.

96. Dan Restrepo, "Migration Doesn't Have to Be a Crisis," *Foreign Affairs*, June 1, 2022, https://www.foreignaffairs.com/articles/americas/2022-06-01/migration-doesnt-have-be-crisis.

97. Susan Fratzke and Andrea Tanco, "Humanitarian Pathways for Central Americans: Assessing Opportunities for the Future," Migration Policy Institute, May 2022, https://www.migrationpolicy.org/research/humanitarian-pathways-central-americans.

98. Claudia Herrera Melgar (executive secretary, Central American Coordination Center for the Prevention of Natural Disasters), in interview with the author, Guatemala City, Guatemala, January 27, 2022.

99. Jeff Ernst et al., "U.S. Foreign Aid to the Northern Triangle 2014–2019: Promoting Success by Learning from the Past," Wilson Center, December 2020, https://www.wilsoncenter.org/sites/default/files/media/uploads/documents/US%20Foreign%20Aid%20Central%20America.pdf.

100. Teresa Romero, "Central Government Debt as Percentage of GDP in Latin America in 2020," Statista, November 2, 2021, https://www.statista.com/statistics/913596/latin-america-caribbean-government-debt-gdp-share.

101. Rubén Ávila García (green finance senior analyst, Central American Economic Integration Bank), in interview with the author, Tegucigalpa, Honduras, May 3, 2022.

102. Benjamin Russell, "How the Business World Can Help Stop Latin America's Violence," *Americas Quarterly*, July 18, 2018, https://www.americasquarterly.org/fulltextarticle/how-the-business-world-can-help-stop-latin-americas-violence.

ACKNOWLEDGMENTS

I am grateful to Paul B. Stares, director of the Center for Preventive Action, for inviting me to join this effort to explore and educate on one of the defining challenges of our lifetimes: the effects of climate change on global stability. I could not have accomplished this project without his support and vision. I am also thankful to the individuals in Central America, Mexico, and the United States who sat for (occasionally long) interviews with me. I hope this paper's argument reflects their collective wisdom and communicates their urgency in addressing the climate crisis in Central America.

I also thank Deputy Director of Studies Shannon O'Neil and Tiziano Breda of the International Crisis Group for the care and interest with which they read and commented on an earlier draft of this paper. Director of Studies James M. Lindsay, Managing Director of Publications Patricia Dorff, Senior Editor Marcelo Agudo, and Research Associate Caroline Kapp provided stellar feedback as well, and I appreciate their advice. Other people who contributed either directly or indirectly to this project and to whom I owe my gratitude include: Senior Fellow for Energy and the Environment Alice Hill, Senior Manager Radmila Jackovich, Studies Grant Management Director Dominic Bocci, David Gevarter, Stephanie Junger-Moat, Carlos Castillo, Lino Miani, Randy Pestana, Felipe Deidan, Jose Pablo Ampudia, Andres Villar, Aliza Asad, and Ellie Estreich. ¡Un millón de gracias!

ABOUT THE AUTHOR

Paul J. Angelo is the director of the William J. Perry Center for Hemispheric Defense Studies at the National Defense University in Washington, DC. He was previously the fellow for Latin America studies and an international affairs fellow at the Council on Foreign Relations. There he focused on U.S.-Latin American relations, transnational crime, security assistance, and immigration. During his tenure as an international affairs fellow, Angelo also represented the U.S. Department of State at the U.S. Embassy in Tegucigalpa, Honduras, where he managed the ambassador's security and justice portfolio. In the Political Section, he provided technical assistance to the Honduran police reform commission; supported strategy development and agenda setting for Afro-descendent, Indigenous, and LGBTQ+ networks to improve civic engagement; and led policy and legal analysis on violence, crime, and migration trends.

Angelo's previous service in the U.S. Navy included tours in a United Kingdom–based North Atlantic Treaty Organization position, on board a destroyer deployed to the Asia-Pacific region, and as an instructor at the U.S. Naval Academy, where he taught Spanish and Latin American politics. During his naval career, Angelo deployed to Colombia on three occasions over the course of more than a decade. During his longest mission in Colombia, he served as the U.S. embassy's principal liaison to the Colombian military and police in the highly conflictive Pacific coast. In 2022, President Joe Biden appointed Angelo to the U.S. Naval Academy board of visitors. He continues to serve as a commander in the U.S. Navy Reserve, supporting the U.S. Naval Forces Southern Command as the executive officer of a Puerto Rico–based unit. He is also the author of a forthcoming book about U.S. security assistance. His written commentary has appeared in *Foreign Affairs*,

Foreign Policy, the *Miami Herald,* the *New York Times,* and the *Washington Post.* Angelo holds a BS in political science from the U.S. Naval Academy, where he was awarded the Harry S. Truman Scholarship, an MPhil in Latin American studies from the University of Oxford, where he studied as a Rhodes Scholar, and a PhD in politics from University College London.

www.ingramcontent.com/pod-product-compliance
Lightning Source LLC
Chambersburg PA
CBHW070818280326
41934CB00012B/3218